EDUCATION AND THE CRISIS IN VALUES: SHOULD WE BE PHILOSOPHICAL ABOUT IT?

THE LONDON FILE - PAPERS FROM THE
INSTITUTE OF EDUCATION

Titles in the series include:

MUSIC EDUCATION AND THE NATIONAL CURRICULUM	Keith Swanwick
WHAT WE KNOW ABOUT EFFECTIVE PRIMARY TEACHING	Caroline Gipps
THE ARTS 5-16: Changing the agenda	John White
MORE HAS MEANT WOMEN: The feminisation of schooling	Jane Miller
NATIONAL CURRICULUM SCIENCE: So near and yet so far	Arthur Jennings
THE PROMISE AND PERILS OF EDUCATIONAL COMPARISON	Martin McLean
THE AIMS OF SCHOOL HISTORY: Has the National Curriculum got it right?	Peter Lee, John Slater, Paddy Walsh and John White
TIME TO CHANGE THE 1981 EDUCATION ACT	Brahm Norwich
A MARKET-LED ALTERNATIVE FOR THE CURRICULUM: Breaking the code	James Tooley
PARTNERSHIP IN INITIAL TEACHER TRAINING: Talk and chalk	Clare Hake
CHANGING LITERACIES: Media education and modern culture	David Buckingham

THE LONDON FILE

PAPERS FROM THE INSTITUTE OF EDUCATION

EDUCATION AND THE CRISIS IN VALUES:

SHOULD WE BE PHILOSOPHICAL ABOUT IT?

GRAHAM HAYDON

INSTITUTE OF EDUCATION
UNIVERSITY OF LONDON

Published by

the Tufnell Press

THE LONDON FILE - PAPERS FROM THE INSTITUTE OF EDUCATION

PUBLISHED
by
the Tufnell Press
47, Dalmeny Road, London, N7 0DY

First published 1993

BRITISH LIBRARY CATALOGUING-IN-PUBLICATION DATA
A catalogue record for this book is available from the British Library

ISBN 1 872767 56 7

Book design by Fiona Barlow, Carter Wong, London
Printed in Great Britain by Da Costa Print, London

CONTENTS

INTRODUCTION	1
IS THERE A CRISIS IN VALUES?	1
PHILOSOPHY AND MORAL LEADERSHIP	6
PHILOSOPHY AND INDIVIDUAL PERPLEXITY ABOUT VALUES	9
PHILOSOPHY AND SOCIETAL PERPLEXITY ABOUT VALUES	12
PHILOSOPHY AND REASONED DISCUSSION ABOUT VALUES	15
PHILOSOPHY IN EDUCATION	19
NOTES	24
REFERENCES	24

Acknowledgments

I have written of a well-established philosophical tradition. To document all of my debts to this tradition would turn this paper into an annotated bibliography. Specifically, though, I would like to thank John White, Patricia White, and an anonymous reader for their comments on earlier drafts.

Introduction

Does society face a crisis in values? And if it does, what should be the response of education? Should we—teachers, theorists, teacher-trainers—shrug our shoulders and resign ourselves philosophically—in one popular sense of the term—to social forces that are outside our power to influence? Or is there something that we can do to enable society better to face its crisis?

I shall argue that philosophy—in another sense of the term, which is more academic but need not be remote from popular understanding—can help us to understand the situation which we may be tempted to describe as a crisis, and, through education, can help society to deal with it. There is a place for a philosophical approach to values, not only in academic philosophy departments, but in the education of teachers and even in the curriculum of our children.

Is There a Crisis in Values?

'Crisis' is a dramatic term, of the sort that lends itself to arresting headlines—and titles. But talk of crisis should not always be taken at face value. Sometimes the sense of some immediate and serious problem, thrusting itself upon us and demanding instant action, is only superficial appearance; more careful analysis may reveal underlying questions of deeper and more lasting importance.

There is a certain picture of the role of values in society which lends itself to talk of a crisis. Values—moral values in particular—are seen as binding society together, preventing the dissolution which might come through individuals pursuing only their own interests or pleasures and disregarding the interests or rights of others. But acknowledgement of values, and adherence to them in action, are depicted as in a state of decline. Education is given the job of reversing the decline. In some versions of this picture—as in the article by John Patten which appeared in *The Spectator* in April 1992, just days after he became Education Secretary—the decline is linked explicitly with the decline in religious belief and observance, and the cure is seen to involve a kind of religious revival, even to the extent of belief in eternal damnation (Patten, 1992).

If this paper were primarily an analysis of the current state of society—which it is not—several questions would have to be raised about this picture. One concerns the nature of the assumed link between religious belief and moral behaviour. Another concerns the tension between two sorts of conservatism: the traditional conservatism (not necessarily linked to a Party) which sees inherited values as the cement of society and is therefore suspicious of any change in values; and the Thatcherite Conservatism which, in its orientation towards individual advancement, seems to many to be part of the problem rather than of the cure. But what is more to the point here is the implicit assumption that there is a unified tradition of values which can serve both as a measure of decline and, via education, as the means of improvement. To speak of decline only makes sense against some assumed standards: *perhaps*, for instance, it is true that there are higher levels of truancy or more juvenile crime. Bringing in other standards, *perhaps* it is also true that more young people than ever before are looking beyond their own interests, are showing an active concern for justice in a wider than national context, for the defence of the weak (including animals), and for the state of the environment. If it were possible to devise a single measure of moral decline or advance, I doubt that one would find a sudden shift just at the present time. But there is an important underlying situation; it is not a matter of moral decline or advance, but the very fact of the plurality of standards to which appeal could be made.

Plurality of standards, that is, of moral values themselves, is not a new phenomenon. The ancient Greek philosophers were well aware of different standards from their own, but they found these primarily within Persia or Egypt rather than in their midst. What has developed increasingly in the modern world is the co-existence of differing values within one society. The causes of this, with reference to a society like Britain, are certainly complex and varied. Immigration and the settling of different ethnic groups is, I think, a relatively minor factor. Independently of ethnic differences, there would be disagreements on such issues as capital punishment, abortion, animal experimentation, the exploitation of natural resources, nuclear deterrence, and many more. And the disagreements are not confined to the means to be used towards agreed ends; rather there is a lack of agreement on the underlying basis on which such issues should be judged. It is not ethnic diversity which underlies such differences as these, but it is perhaps a diversity of moral traditions (cf. MacIntyre, 1981). Diversity of moral traditions does have some link with diversity of religious traditions, and the latter, of course, goes back for centuries within Britain. So far as diversity of values is concerned, the main contribution of ethnic diversity in recent times has probably been in extending the diversity of religions. For some of the seemingly most intractable of recent disputes on questions of values, such as the abortion issue, or the disputes around the publication of *The Satanic Verses*, have turned on differences between religions, or between religious and secular viewpoints.[1]

An underlying plurality of values, then, has not suddenly come upon us. What is, perhaps, a more recent change is the extent to which the diversity has become public. This may be partly the result of wider dissemination of information through the mass media, and of the extension of education which has, only in historically recent times, far enlarged the public forum in which morally charged issues are aired. Whatever the explanations, the fact is that the plurality is now, and surely irreversibly, 'in the open'. It is no longer possible for society to get by on the assumption that really there is homogeneity of moral outlook, give or take a few heretics or deviants, who can be ostracised or otherwise marginalised. Moral plurality stares us in the face; but, from an historical perspective, we seem to be still at the stage of recognising this and having to adjust to it.

One symptom of our still having to make this adjustment, I suggest, is that it remains easy for the expression of differences in values to be read as evidence of decline. In the treatment of the terminally ill, for instance, what to some will seem an advance in terms both of rationality and of compassion—allowing at least passive euthanasia, with the consent of next of kin, for patients being kept alive only by artificial means and in a vegetative state—will to others be further evidence of a decline in respect for human life. And many Muslim objectors to *The Satanic Verses* will have seen its publication as an extreme instance of the secularism for which, literally, nothing is sacred; while for some of the defenders of Rushdie any indication of deference towards Muslim values was seen as a step backwards away from hard-won liberal freedoms. To the extent that a society lacks a shared sense of underlying values, it must lack a shared sense even of whether perceived change of values constitutes an improvement or a decline. There is a permanent possibility, then, that any change will be seen by at least some members of society as a decline.

Apart from the unease, or worse, which some people will feel at what they perceive as a decline in moral standards, is a plurality of moral outlooks within a society necessarily a bad thing? In itself, probably not, but some of its effects may be. Most obviously, there are cases in which it leads to conflict which can involve violence or the threat of violence.[2] More indirectly, it is *possible* that perceived plurality of standards does contribute something towards lessened respect for morality—towards people's being less concerned about whether their behaviour does conform to moral standards or not. For the perceived plurality leads some people to the kind of relativism or subjectivism which says that it is all just a matter of opinion: and this might (though it need not) lead to the further thought that it can not, after all, matter very much what one does. It is possible, then, that plurality of standards does contribute something to moral decline in this way, independently of the particular standards in question; though the connection is by no means established. What can rather more confidently be expected is that the perceived plurality leads to a lack of faith in moral discussion. If there are no common standards or arguments to which to appeal when issues like those listed above become prominent, the tendency will be for groups adhering to different standards to do little more—to be able to do little more—than continue to exchange, and in the process perhaps to magnify, their differences.

It is this point, and not an alleged general decline in standards of behaviour, that should be of special concern to educators. If there is a general decline, the influences leading to it are inevitably many and varied, and may, for all we know, have much of their effect on children before they ever come into contact with teachers. If teachers are being held responsible for a general decline in standards of behaviour, they may well be right to protest at the ills of society being blamed on them. But, in contrast, if the plurality of moral standards and outlooks means that there are conflicts in society which can only be settled at best by the counting of preferences through the ballot box (which is still a rather crude way of settling a moral dispute) and at worst by violence, *but not, in either case, through reasoned discussion*, this is especially a concern for formal education, since no other institution than the school in society is likely to do much to promote the tendency and the capacity to turn to rational argument rather than merely to the assertion of one position against another.

Does the situation I have described constitute a crisis? Not perhaps if that word always carries connotations of a sudden dramatic event. But if a crisis is a turning point in human affairs which calls for important judgements to be made, then within a longer historical perspective we are living through a crisis. It is the turning point to which observers and participants—and we all play both roles—have been responding in a variety of ways, from the politicians' call for the reassertion of traditional values in teaching, to the occasional but newsworthy controversies among parents of different cultural or religious backgrounds about their children's schooling, to the academic debates about modernism and postmodernism.

In this essay I want to ask whether philosophy can offer a way through the crisis. One kind of response to that question, which has a history going back to Plato in the West and Confucius in the East, is to look to philosophy itself to provide moral leadership. If people have lost their way in perplexity over values, it is for philosophy to set up the beacon which the travellers can aim at—and it will be for education to ensure that they do not stray from the path. But if, as I shall argue, philosophy cannot have this role, then if it is to help at all it must be not so much a beacon, as part of the equipment by which people find their own way. Rather than guiding people's lives from outside, philosophy will have to enter into people's own thinking—and this will mean a quite different relationship between philosophy and education. There is a long history of philosophers making recommendations about education—and since I am myself writing as a philosopher of education, I cannot avoid playing that role myself. But what I want to say in that role is that if philosophy confines itself to making recommendations for education from the outside, it will be doing much less than it might do. There is a place for philosophy in education, not merely in offering a commentary on it.

I do not want to suggest that educationalists have not already been trying to come to terms with the plurality of values in our society. Nineteen ninety two saw, for instance, the twenty-fifth anniversary of one of the best-known initiatives in tackling controversial issues of values in schools: the Schools Council/Nuffield Humanities Curriculum Project. As is—or was—well-known, a central methodological tenet of the project was that the teacher should take the role of neutral chairperson in discussions of controversial issues. This proposal itself proved highly controversial, for there were those who thought that the teacher had a responsibility to take a stand on the issues that divided society, giving a lead by example and by argument. Philosophers engaged in the debate on both sides (cf. Bridges, 1979:118-127; Hare, 1992). And more widely, outside the confines of that particular debate, philosophers have always been among those who have had recommendations to make for education in values in a society where few values can be taken for granted (cf. Cochrane, Hamm and Kazepides (eds.), 1979; Peters, 1981; Straughan, 1982; Wilson, 1990). But there have been no recommendations, philosophical or otherwise, which have met with sufficiently general approval to be widely implemented. The questions are still with us, and there is still room for more to be said. While I shall be following here the tradition of seeking to apply philosophy to educational questions, I shall be arguing more specifically that, if philosophy is to be of practical relevance to the wider social context that I have identified, it is people more generally, not just professional philosophers, who will have to apply it.

Philosophy and Moral Leadership

If philosophy professes to appeal, not to revelation or tradition or authority, but simply to reason, it ought to be philosophy that could set up a standard above the existing conflict of values. As is well known, for Plato, we would achieve the ideal society (which includes harmony among the different sections of the population), if we had philosophers as rulers, who would see what is good and right and direct society accordingly. But such an answer is not available now, if it ever was. It depends on at least three assumptions: that there is an objective truth, accessible to reason, about what is good and right; that philosophers, with the proper training, will achieve the wisdom to see what that answer is; and that there is the possibility within society of philosophers possessing acknowledged authority.

The first of these assumptions is one, of course, about which many people are now sceptical, but it is by no means universally rejected. It is not the lack of objectively right answers (if they are lacking) that makes Plato's answer unavailable now; it is the fact (contrary to the second assumption) that even philosophers cannot agree on what the answers are. A modern Platonist might try to save the second assumption by claiming that most of the philosophers have got it wrong because they have not had the right philosophical training; but philosophers would not agree on which form of training was right any more than they agree on final answers. The fact of disagreement is no proof that there might not be agreement at some future time, but it does not inspire confidence, and in any case there are practical tasks for society, and especially for teachers, which can hardly wait on such a possibility.

In any case the third assumption is yet another obstacle. Among the traditions of thought and practice in our society, there are some that are firmly enough entrenched, even if not undisputed, to rule out the political form of Plato's solution; for one thing, put briefly, it is undemocratic. And apart from constitutional form, there is a widespread, though not universal, sense that especially in moral matters it is better that people should think for themselves and not simply be told what to do. This sense is strong especially in educational thought; which is why educationalists, however devoted to reason, could not accept without qualms the idea of philosophy having political authority.

There might, of course, be other ways in which philosophers could exercise influence without having authority. There is, for instance, an increasing body of applied philosophy, bringing philosophical methods and insights to bear on issues of practical moral concern. Is it, perhaps, in such work as this—not through public pronouncements of what is to be done, but through careful and piecemeal dissection of problems—that philosophers will contribute to resolving perplexity about values and policy in our society?

This is partly right, but the limits of such a contribution must be recognised. For one thing, in applying their skills in a relatively piecemeal way 'applied philosophers' will most often leave the underlying moral complexion of society as it is. They may apply some particular moral theory (which might itself be disputed among moral philosophers); they may appeal to some presumed consensus, for instance on certain liberal-democratic principles; they may even let the argument rest at some point on their own 'intuitive' sense of what is right. They will not necessarily converge amongst themselves on the same solution; philosophers do not stand outside society, but themselves share in society's plurality of values.

There is a sense, too, in which applied philosophers are still 'theorists'. The majority of what is written by applied philosophers is published in academic journals or books, and is read chiefly by other philosophers and students of philosophy. The term 'applied philosophy' picks out a branch of the subject in much the same way as 'applied mathematics' picks out a branch of mathematics. A girl who is sitting in a classroom doing calculations about the stresses in bridges would be doing applied mathematics; but in another sense she is not applying mathematics at all, if her calculations never have any practical effect outside the classroom or even within it. (Contrast the case in which her calculations are put to use in the making of some item of equipment which will actually be used in the school.) Similarly, applied philosophy may be an area which many students of the subject wish to study, but in studying it they are not necessarily applying philosophy.

The idea that applied philosophy is 'applied' in too academic a sense seems also to have struck the writer of this letter to the editors of the *Journal of Applied Philosophy* (3 (2) 1986:286):

> Dear Editors,
>
> Intrigued by a reference to your journal I borrowed a copy, number 2 of 1985. I was disappointed.
>
> Your journal has full references, good English and rich arguments but seems confined to a highbrow audience who have years of academic practice, access to specialist books and financial support to ruminate over areas of personal interest. I expect, in a *Journal of Applied Philosophy*, to find examples of philosophers using their subject to help other people solve problems: in a classroom, factory, dentist's surgery or urban semi. This is the challenge. You must put your heads together and produce something practical which the man in the street can use—a personal lifeline for turbulent times.

There may be many people who, having looked with hope to see what philosophy could provide, have shared this writer's frustration; and these may include some teachers who have been disappointed in the hope that philosophy of education would give them a lifeline for survival in the classroom, or even in the staffroom. Nevertheless, though one can sympathise, what this letter writer asks for is not what philosophers should be trying to provide. Because they do not agree amongst themselves, and because they lack acknowledged authority, philosophers can not be throwers of lifelines. That metaphor suggests that the person to whom the line is thrown is relatively passive—able to splash and shout, perhaps, but otherwise only able to cling on and be pulled to safety. Even if the times are perceived as ones of crisis, this can hardly be the model which educationalists and democrats could endorse. That philosophy, if it is to offer something to the person in the street, cannot be confined to academic journals, is certainly true; but philosophers are not throwers of lifelines. Just possibly, they might be swimming instructors.

Philosophy and Individual Perplexity About Values

In effect, I have been saying that philosophers cannot do people's thinking for them (a point which could be supported from within a number of traditions of thought, philosophical, political and religious). Does this mean that, if philosophy is to be of any help in the resolution of perplexity about values, everyone should be a philosopher? And should education take that as one of its aims?

Stated baldly, such an aim would seem absurdly ambitious. But there is more than a germ of sense in it. In the first place, whatever else philosophers may be, they are—in intention, and to a degree in reality—people who think critically: who do not take assertions for granted, who question presuppositions, test the validity of arguments, and so on. That people should come to be critical thinkers is not an esoteric aim for education, indeed it is a widely shared one. There are many now who advocate that formal education should include courses in critical thinking as a distinct skill; there are many others who, perhaps sceptical of the idea that critical thinking can be a subject in itself, nevertheless would want whatever is taught to be taught in such a way as to encourage a critical approach. At any rate, critical thinking is clearly not something exclusive to philosophy. It can still be asked whether education, for everyone, ought to try to borrow some of the subject matter, and not just the methods, of philosophy.

Our concern here is with perplexity about values. If people are to be able to think for themselves in matters of values, it is not enough that they be capable of critical thought in a general way; for such thinking can often, by itself, have a predominantly negative effect. That is, the critical thinker about values may be led only to a sceptical conclusion—that there is no clear warrant for any particular position. This would only reinforce the perceived fact of diversity of standards which was our starting point; and if this was all philosophy could do it would be part of the problem, not of the solution. It does not, in our society, take much independence of thought to be aware of diversity in values; but faced with diversity and uncertainty, there is a need for individuals to be able to think for themselves. This is why there is a reason in a pluralist society for people to be positively encouraged to think critically, even if that reason would be less salient from within the perspective of a single and relatively homogeneous tradition (cf. the kind of justification of the value of autonomy offered by Raz, 1986 p. 391 and White, 1990 pp. 103-4). We need to ask, then, whether philosophy can make some positive contribution to a person's ability to cope with diversity of values.

But at the same time, we would surely be disappointed if the conclusion were that philosophy could make its contribution provided only that it could turn people into moral philosophers: as if everyone might be equipped to settle fundamental questions about values which have exercised philosophers for thousands of years and in many cultures.

Can we look to philosophy to fill any role between, on the one hand, providing answers which others are expected merely to follow, and on the other hand, seeking to turn everyone into a philosopher? Fortunately, there is a sense in which an individual, using the resources of philosophy (among others), may come to a resolution of perplexity without claiming to have solved universal problems. An individual may use what the American political philosopher John Rawls (1972:20) has called the method of 'reflective equilibrium'. This is not a form of argument which attempts to take nothing for granted; rather, it assumes that those who are able and disposed to think for themselves about questions of values do already have certain value commitments. These will be more or less firmly held, and will be at different levels. Some, like the idea of respect for life, will be at a very general level; others, like opposition to capital punishment, will be more specific; still others may be specific to a particular instance—as that, whatever the general principles might be, execution of this person for this offence cannot be right. Clearly there are possibilities of tension between different value commitments—as when the democrat opposed to capital punishment recognises that majority decision making would lead to the opposite conclusion.

Rawls' idea of reflective equilibrium sets up an aim for the rational thinker to try to achieve, starting from this kind of position, and taking neither general principles nor specific commitments as sacrosanct. The aim is to have in the end a set of principles, and a set of 'intuitions' about particular cases, which fit each other without incoherence. The fit is to be achieved, not by adopting a set of principles with a quite independent justification and then changing one's intuitions to fit; but also not by thinking up a theory which will fit all of the individual's specific intuitions willy-nilly (these specific intuitions might in any case turn out not to be consistent with each other). Rather, there will be a process of adjustment at each end. When the fit is achieved the individual's moral thinking is in the state that Rawls calls 'reflective equilibrium'.

Now those who feel in a quandary about values might well feel less bewildered if they had at least got their own value commitments into such a condition. And there is no doubt that to achieve this would need a process of thinking which would be far from irrational, and which could be facilitated by ideas and terminology which philosophers, among others, have brought into moral debate. (In this way, the idea of aiming at reflective equilibrium goes beyond the idea of 'values clarification', if that means simply getting clear about the values one is starting from; cf. Pring, 1984:75-6). To enable individuals, then, to think their way through to a condition of reflective equilibrium is one way in which philosophy may be able to offer support to the layperson 'in turbulent times'.

Of course, it would be optimistic to assume that a person would always manage to find a point of reflective equilibrium. For if at the beginning the individual has intuitions which pull in different ways, the result of reflection may be only that the intuitions have been sharpened up, while the tension remains. And this will be the point at which, if action is called for, a decision will still have to be made. But this is only to say that a point can come when individuals have to take responsibility for a decision despite uncertainty—though they might like to turn to someone else for a lifeline, in doing so they might be only substituting someone else's point of reflective equilibrium for that which they have failed to find for themselves.

The method of reflective equilibrium, then, perhaps more than Rawls recognises, is one for individuals to apply for themselves. In a perfectly good sense, it enables a person to get to a resolution of a problem which is 'right for her or himself'. That phrase may be anathema to anti-relativists, but it has here a sense which is not committed to relativism (since it does not pass judgment on whether incompatible sets of beliefs can all be true). The point is only that individuals, as a matter of fact, start with different sets of commitments and beliefs, and different balances between what they are more or less sure about, so that the particular complex of value positions which might be a point of reflective equilibrium for one person might not be so for another.

Now in one respect this fact is in line with the climate of our times. An application of philosophy which allows different people to come to different answers fits with the pluralism of our culture. Yet, by the same token, while it may be consistent with this pluralism, it does not offer a resolution of the problems which the diversity of standards raises on a social rather than individual level. It is this level to which we must now turn.

Philosophy and Societal Perplexity About Values

In looking at the individual application of philosophy we have so far neglected the extent to which moral decisions have to be capable of public discussion and defence. To see this, consider the kind of moral dilemma which a doctor or nurse may face in deciding, say, how to treat a terminally ill but mentally alert patient. The practitioner, though perhaps starting with conflicting intuitions and principles, may be able to get to a state of reflective equilibrium and hence feel comfortable with the decision made. And this will certainly count for something. But other people, including the patient, may have their own different convictions, and can still challenge the practitioner to justify the decision to them. Even if practitioner and patient agree (which might be sufficient basis for taking a particular line of action in a given case), this agreement can still be open to challenge within a wider constituency.

In such a case one person may try to justify his or her decision to others. A justification of a decision cannot be simply a re-assertion of it; nor can it be merely the stating of an argument which appears valid to the person stating it. For in the sense that is relevant here, a justification is a justification to others, and does not succeed unless it is recognised as a justification by others. Therefore it has to take into account the position from which others start, has to address their concerns, and cannot ride roughshod over their convictions, even if it does not accept them. It will respect the fact that participants start from different positions; that each has convictions, some more general, some more specific, and that any of these may be more or less firmly held; that for any person there may be some things which are sticking points, but at the same time there may be a desire for coherence and lack of 'cognitive dissonance'.

A discussion in which the participants mutually recognise these factors will be one in which each may be willing to modify his or her position to some extent, in the hope that a consensus might be reached (though not at any cost). In other words, such a discussion would be very like the process of trying to reach reflective equilibrium, but with a collective rather than individual scope. Indeed, it could be analogous to the process which many philosophical writers on morality have used. An individual philosopher will often take into account, without treating as sacrosanct, his or her own intuitions about moral value, and also those of other people so far as these are known. This is something that can also be done collectively, and can in fact be done all the more effectively as a co-operative endeavour, in that rather than assumptions being made about other people's intuitions, people will be feeding their own intuitions directly into the process. Where a professional philosopher might conclude by recommending a theory as a reasonable one for people to adopt, people in discussion might reach a conclusion which they themselves can feel is a reasonable one for them to adopt—even though they may not have agreed on everything along the way. And since this would be a conclusion they had reached for themselves, rather than one taken at second hand, it would be all the more likely that they would take it seriously.

Of course, a process of discussion about moral positions will often fail to lead to consensus; but, even then, something may have been gained from the attempt. Consider again the analogy with the one-person case. Though the individual in the end might—if action is demanded—have to make a decision, without a lifeline to grasp, still she or he will make that decision with greater understanding; it may even, in at least some respects, be a better decision because of this understanding. And that same point could hold for a group or even a whole society. Often decisions have to be made which stand on behalf of a group and are binding on them—some of these are decisions which we count as political, and they may be arrived at with little discussion, simply by one point of view numerically outweighing another. In the nature of such decisions, they will not carry everyone with them; but at least we can say that if the decisions have been made on the basis of discussion, after a serious attempt to see where the differences are and whether any reconciliation is possible, then they may be better decisions in the sense that more people may be able to accept that they are, in the circumstances, justifiable; and those who have not themselves endorsed the conclusion may have gained a greater understanding of what has led to it.

Since I am here talking about the conditions of reasoned discussion of values within a plural society, I should recognise the challenge of those who believe that there is very little scope for such discussion. Alasdair MacIntyre (1987) has argued that there can be no such thing as an educated public in a modern society. There can only, he claims, be an educated public if a significant part of the population has been educated in a common intellectual tradition, which will give to public debate common standards for the rational assessment of questions of values. Only within such common standards can there be rational discussion. In the sense in which he uses the term, MacIntyre is right that we cannot now hope to produce an educated public, since we cannot educate the population in a single philosophical tradition which will provide the criteria for deciding questions in public debate.

We cannot have a public educated in, say, utilitarian philosophy, or Kantianism, or for that matter in a Protestant or Catholic or Judaic or Islamic moral tradition—not because such an education is in principle impossible (for my argument I can leave it an open question whether there could be education, rather than indoctrination, in a specific moral framework) but because we could not, in our pluralist society, have agreement on one particular tradition as the one to be transmitted.

But if it is true that the parties to a discussion which is regulated by the idea of trying to reach reflective equilibrium need not all be adherents of the same tradition, this does not mean that they have no scope for rational discussion. That they do not share some of their fundamental substantive values does not mean that they could not share a vocabulary. Indeed, it would be essential that they should have a degree of sophistication in their concepts and terminology. My suggestion is that there is a tradition which can provide a common vocabulary, and that people could be educated within this. This is not specifically the utilitarian or Kantian or scholastic tradition, or some other, but the very tradition of trying to think in a systematic way about the moral questions that matter to individuals and their society. MacIntyre, of course, would not accept that this would be an education within a tradition in the sense he has in mind, for this broad tradition of thinking does not have the internal coherence to offer determinate and unitary standards for the rational evaluation of competing positions. But if we were to think of the goal as being not to find a set of principles which could be acknowledged as being correct in the light of a single coherent tradition—still less in the light of all of them—but as being, if possible, to find resolutions of practical questions which people are willing to endorse for practical purposes; and failing that, at least to achieve a greater understanding of the reasons for the differences, then the broader tradition of philosophical thinking about values could be an invaluable aid, not least as it has already within itself taken account of and developed a variety of views.

Philosophy and Reasoned Discussion About Values

To give now a little more detail, I shall argue that philosophy can contribute to the conditions for more reasonable and informed discussion about values in at least three ways: no doubt there are overlaps between these, and further possibilities too.

1. First, philosophy could contribute to a more systematic study of morality as a phenomenon than is common within our education system. Given the importance of moral beliefs and practices in the lives both of individuals and of society, it can appear surprising that morality is not often itself a direct topic of attention within education. (It does not, for instance, have the disciplinary status of Economics or Politics, though it might arguably be seen as more fundamental to human life than either of these.) Perhaps the phenomenon of morality is both too fundamental and too all-pervading to have been separated out in this way as a distinct field of study. And many people perhaps would not see it as a fit object for systematic enquiry—but for a variety of reasons. To some, it is essentially a personal matter, a sphere ultimately of subjective choice, and for that reason not subject to generalisation. For others it may be a concrete social code whose main prescriptions are simply not in doubt. But to others again it may seem to have a certain mysteriousness, from which too objectifying a study might detract. For many, it is inextricably associated with religion, and is to be studied in that connection. The intimate relation which does hold for many people between their religious belief and their morality is one that, in a plural and liberal society, has to be taken seriously. The implications of this for education within a secular society will have to be explored elsewhere (cf. Haydon, 1993). But since it is also true, in a plural and liberal society, that a link between morality and religion cannot be taken for granted, it cannot be right to suppose that within schools morality should be the concern exclusively of Religious Education.

The existence of such a variety of conceptions of the nature of morality—which can co-exist, not merely in one society but within one tradition, and even in the thinking of one individual—suggests that attempts at serious discussion of values may well find themselves at cross purposes if the attention of all pupils is not directed to the different ways in which the phenomenon of morality can be realised in people's experience. It may be experienced, for instance, as a realm of individual and apparently arbitrary choice; as a system of demands made by the powerful within society; as the dictates of impersonal reason; as a matter of deep emotional commitment; as the demands of a stern, or of a loving, God.

I would make no claim that philosophy is the only discipline relevant to an understanding of morality in all its manifestations; clearly this list already suggests that psychology, sociology and theology could all be relevant. But philosophy, as a tradition of enquiry which is not committed to the perspectives of any one of these, and which is more concerned with the uncovering and clarification of presuppositions than it is with empirical evidence, would have an important role in seeing that one perspective does not come to hold the field to the neglect of others. Perhaps most importantly, the resources of the philosophical tradition can help to guard against too easy an acceptance, either of the fundamentalist kind of objectivism which does not see any room for reasonable people to hold different points of view, or of the anti-rational kind of relativism which would have it that there is no scope for reasoned criticism of any views (cf. Wilson, 1990, ch.2).

2. One important aspect of morality is the area of policy on matters of public moral concern (of which some examples were mentioned above). Moral and political philosophy can offer a rich set of resources for understanding and articulating possibilities. At this level, precisely because it is a public one, any one position on a particular issue carries with it presuppositions which, if they were articulated, would amount to a more general theory about how moral questions are to be decided. And it is rarely that people will come up with some new theory, not already explored in one or another of the existing strands of philosophical enquiry. A great many debates, for instance, carry recognisably the marks of a utilitarian or of a Kantian position. To be able to see what kind of position oneself or another is holding; to be able to appreciate that, because of the nature of one's background and implicit theory, any positions will have implications beyond the particular case; to be able to ask whether one finds these broader implications acceptable; to be aware of a range of arguments on just these questions which have already been explored and do not have to be invented anew; all this is an aid to public discussion with understanding.

The same might be said about conceptions within political philosophy on such matters as the principles of social justice, the legitimacy of the state, the authority of law and the extent and limits of toleration. It should be clear from what was said earlier that it is not being advocated here that the public should simply follow the prescriptions of philosophers. These are all matters for public debate; but even the simple principle of not re-inventing the wheel would suggest that the debate should be informed by the resources which philosophy can make available. (It need hardly be said that the suggestion is not that dogmas should be inculcated or techniques taught and used in a mechanical way; knowing what previous thinkers have come up with, when this can itself be subjected to scrutiny, is an enhancement of the possibilities of autonomous participation in discussion, not a constraint.)

Here, too, belongs the clarification that philosophy can offer on the possibility of maintaining a distinction between morality and law. Not all traditions may draw this distinction in the same way; but for a society in which it will be possible for a diversity of values to co-exist it is vital that it can be drawn. On this distinction rests the recognition that the fact that a certain moral conviction is held is not by itself a sufficient argument for that conviction being enshrined in law; and this recognition is in turn essential if the conclusion of public debate over matters of moral concern is not going to be simply the imposition of power by one group over others (see also the reference to Ackerman below). But these points are perhaps not as widely appreciated as philosophers and political theorists might hope; it is in the course of formal education that the groundwork for understanding them would have to be laid.

3. Reasoned discussion is a matter of form and not only of content. Discussion of issues can too often take the form of no more than a reciprocal assertion of points of view. This is true of a good deal of political debate and even of debate in educational contexts. The point at which people express commitment to different values need not be the terminus of discussion—sometimes it may be only the starting point for it. But if there is to be serious discussion on public moral issues, education must lay the groundwork. And the somewhat artificial conditions of the classroom should make it possible for students to acquire a sense of the difference between discussion and simple exchange of views.

The idea of discussion which aims at mutual agreement is a better model here than the idea of a debate in which it is difference rather than common ground that is emphasised. This is why something like the idea of achieving reflective equilibrium, even if it were never realised in practice, could be a useful regulatory concept. And again, the philosophical tradition contains rich seams that can be mined for ideas which can help to give an appropriate structure to discussion. It does not matter if such ideas are used eclectically: the aim, educationally speaking, would not be that a discussion should reflect accurately the intentions of this particular philosopher or that. Rather, the conditions of discussion should be ones which the participants themselves can recognise as fair and reasonable; but, again, there is no need to re-invent all that has been anticipated and articulated by philosophical writers (cf. Bridges, 1979).

One might, for instance, draw on ideas developed by Habermas (e.g. 1990a, 1990b) about the constraints that must be recognised in discourse if it is to lead to a consensus in which no force but the force of the better argument will ultimately prevail. Parties to such discourse have to accept that whatever they say can be subject to challenge (and the challenges in turn subject to the same constraints); for Habermas, utterances can be challenged with respect to their intelligibility, their truth (or, if they involve normative claims, the validity of these claims, which for Habermas is analogous to truth), their sincerity, and their appropriateness to the situation. All of these can be relevant in discussion, and to recognise the differences between them is already a step towards reasonable discussion.

Challenges to the normative validity of claims are, of course, going to be central in debates about values. Often, there is a background of values implicitly shared against which challenges may be made; but once the question of normative validity is explicitly raised, appealing to an assumed background is no longer sufficient. Nor can it be sufficient for participants to rest their case on simple assertion. One could borrow here from the account of liberal discourse developed by Ackerman (1980). He is considering discourse intended to justify the possession of power; his analysis is relevant here because the claims of a dominant group to have moral correctness on their side on an issue of public moral concern can often be translated, through law or simply through public opinion, into the exercise of constraint over others. In Ackerman's account, among other conditions, claiming that one's own conception of the good is better than that of other citizens is not a good reason in attempting to justify the exercise of power over others. The point intended is not that it is wrong for someone to make such a claim; members of a religious community, for instance, may believe that their conception of the good is better than that of their fellow citizens, and they may say so. But within a reasoned discussion such an assertion will not have weight in justifying policy decisions unless it can be justified by reasons acceptable to others who do not share the same presuppositions (cf. Haydon, 1993).

If there is to be critique and justification of moral claims across divisions within a pluralist society, appeal must be made to ideas which can be widely shared. The tradition of moral philosophy has examined many such forms of argument. To take one of the most significant examples, the challenge: 'What if everyone did that?' is likely to be within the repertoire of anyone in our society. But as it stands, this challenge is open to too many differing interpretations and counter-claims, such as 'Everyone won't, so it won't matter if a few people do'. In serious discussion, such challenges and responses would not be simply rhetorical moves; participants would be able to discuss, in the particular case, whether such a challenge and response are relevant or not. An awareness of the clarifications and distinctions made by philosophers such as R. M. Hare (1981) on the notion of universalisability of moral judgments would be of great value here. If not in the background knowledge of all parties to the discussion, it might at least be within the knowledge of those who try to facilitate discussion, including teachers in the classroom.

Philosophy in Education

Though there has been space only for a few examples, I have been arguing that if education is to help us in dealing with the plurality of values with which we have to live, there should be some injection of philosophical elements into education itself. Is there any practical possibility of this? That there should, within formal education, be some systematic study of moral values as both a personal and social concern, and that this study should be informed by ideas and methods drawn from philosophy, is a policy that could sensibly be advocated as in the national interest. It is not inconceivable that, at some future time, a government might take such a policy on board. For the moment, any implementation of the suggestions made would have to fit within curriculum constraints that are largely determined by the National Curriculum. There would be little mileage in seeking to add a new subject to an already over-crowded curriculum. Even if this could be done, it would risk the subject being seen, misleadingly, as detached from other concerns within the curriculum. The way forward, rather, would have to be within existing areas of curricular concern. It would not be within the scope of this essay to make detailed recommendations, but some possible pointers can be given, using again the three headings from the last section.[3]

1. First, to focus at times on morality itself, taking into account the various ways in which moral values may be experienced by the individual, and how there is interaction in both directions between this individual experience and broader social factors, is perhaps no more than an extension of work that is already done in some of the more systematically planned secondary courses in Personal and Social Education. Since such courses, probably more than any other area of the curriculum, are likely to work best when those who will be teaching them are involved in their planning, there should be no attempt to lay down a single way of getting into the issues. But since much of the work that is done with adolescents within programmes of Personal and Social Education already focuses on the choices which individuals have to make, a likely starting point will be the ways (which may vary between individuals) in which values of various sorts enter into decision making. Not all values are moral values; the next step, then, may be to explore what is involved in recognising certain sorts of concern as moral. Given the beginnings of a sense of what might mark off moral concerns from others (and even at the cost of greater messiness, this is surely something to be drawn out from the understandings which individuals bring with them, rather than to be laid down by the teacher), it can be asked where these concerns come from and what sort of force they have. The aim will not be to arrive at a definitive answer; there is positive value in an awareness of a range of answers, both for the sake of mutual understanding, and, as was suggested above, to guard against too easy an acceptance of one kind of answer as 'obvious'. Teachers will need some awareness of differences which show partial correlations with differences of gender (cf. Gilligan, Ward and Taylor,1988), of cultural background and of religious faith or the lack of it; and as often, philosophy can help to clarify the import of differences on which there is empirical evidence.

2. Complementary to the approach just considered, is to start from particular issues of personal and public concern which will have a place in the curriculum in their own right, and to draw out and make explicit the kinds of moral question which are raised in discussions of these issues. The recent thinking of the National Curriculum Council has, in effect, categorised a variety of such issues under the cross-curricular themes of Education for Economic and Industrial Understanding, Health Education, Careers Education, Environmental Education, and Education for Citizenship. So long as this particular listing of themes has a certain official—though not statutory—standing, it may well be useful to work within it. But even apart from NCC pronouncements, there are surely issues here which most schools already recognise as ones which need to be addressed. I would not want to suggest

that the issues raised should be seen purely as moral ones; but what can be urged is that when a school considers how it is to approach such issues, the opportunities for cross comparison of the moral issues raised should not be missed. It would not only tend towards unnecessary duplication of effort, it would also be misleading to pupils, if a variety of areas of concern were each seen as calling up quite distinctive sets of values. Utilitarian thinking, for instance—and opposition to it as well—will crop up whether the context is one of the environment, the economy, the political system, or issues of personal conduct (cf. Haydon,1992).

While the issues of most concern at a given time may change, and new information and developments in theory will become relevant, certain ways of approaching questions of values do tend to persist. Since the kinds of issues in question come up for discussion in the political forum, it could be argued that developing an ability to recognise these approaches should be part of education for citizenship in particular; and it should be stressed that 'education for citizenship' should be seen not as an add-on extra but as an essential part of the education of everyone within a plural society. Already in the primary school many of the issues, and many of the different perspectives available on them, are likely to be in evidence. It will be useful here for teachers to have the capacity to recognise the kinds of position that children are taking up. In the secondary school, more specifically philosophical content could be introduced, such as the terminology by which pupils themselves could be enabled pick out and compare different approaches.

3. The third point raised above concerned the form of reasoned discussion. Discussion of issues is familiar enough in both primary and secondary schools; less common, perhaps, is an explicit recognition of systematic constraints on discussion. Though reference was made above to the ideas of certain writers, it is not suggested that these should be used simply as rules to be imposed on the conduct of discussions. It would be essential that participants should understand the reasons for the constraints; though this is not incompatible with rules being laid down by the teacher, it is more likely to come about where constraints are arrived at by the participants themselves on the basis of experience. The same group might well make various attempts at formulating rules to govern their own discussions; they will not themselves need to be able to recognise the respects in which their own conclusions may have been anticipated by theorists. It will nevertheless be valuable for the teacher to have some knowledge of the kinds of

constraints which have been advocated by philosophers, and thus to be able to suggest possibilities which might not occur to pupils unaided.

Since occasions for the discussion of values are not confined to one aspect of school life or one part of the curriculum, all teachers, and especially secondary teachers, would ideally be equipped to undertake the kind of work suggested. I must consider finally, then, what can be done towards this goal. Though there is now much scepticism about the role of theory in teacher education, it would be a mistake to see the present proposal as something that has been tried and found wanting. Many courses of initial teacher training have in the past contained elements of philosophy, with the intention that such elements would help to make the trainees more reflective teachers. The judgement, with hindsight, that such courses did relatively little, *by comparison with practical classroom experience*, to improve teaching quality, may well be justified. Part of the reason for failure was that beginning teachers, by and large, had relatively little teaching experience on which to reflect. It is now often found that teachers returning to study after a few years in the classroom get far more out of philosophy of education.

But the proposal now being made is not for philosophy of education, but for other elements of the philosophical tradition, chiefly drawn from moral and political philosophy. Since trainee teachers are moral beings and citizens, and have been living all their lives in a social world partly constituted by moral values, they will not lack experience on which to reflect. I shall develop elsewhere the suggestion that it may be especially in the area of equal opportunities (which is, of course, important in its own right) that teachers will find ample material for reflecting both on shared values and conflicts of values.

It has to be recognised, however, that the near future of initial teacher training, on any likely scenario, will be one in which there is relatively little time for giving trainee teachers an acquaintance with philosophical ideas (cf. Haydon,1992). Whatever is done may have to be done, initially at least, in a less systematic way through in-service work. There are teachers who, having at least an inkling of the kind of illumination that the philosophical tradition can offer on questions which are in any case inescapable, will choose (if they have the choice) to follow philosophical courses. If they and their pupils benefit from this, the benefits will eventually be seen more widely, and it may gradually become possible to extend the relevant philosophical input more widely through teacher education. If the results of such developments are not to be too fragmentary, it will be important for a sense of overall purpose to be kept in mind. In a plural society it is doubtful whether it should be seen as the business of education to transmit a common culture in a full-blooded sense; and we could not expect every teacher to be in possession of such a culture. It may be the business of education, though, to pass on to new generations, and indeed to spread more widely, a common basis of discourse within which diversities can be understood and accommodated. It can still be possible for teachers to have command of this, provided their own education is not to be confined entirely to specialist subjects and on-the-job skills.

Notes

1 In this work I am concentrating on the contribution which can be made by a philosophical tradition which is itself predominantly secular. But it is not part of my position that non-secular viewpoints should be excluded from public discussion of moral issues (cf. Haydon,1993).

2 That violence is better avoided is itself, of course, a value judgement, but one that is probably more widely shared than many. I have explored the ways in which differences in values can lead to overt conflict between persons in a forthcoming report on Education and Peace for the Oxford Project for Peace Studies.

3 I am not trying to say here all that could be said, even from the point of view of philosophy, about the total contribution that good schools, through their ethos and in other ways, can make to the moral development of young people; I am arguing for the important place of philosophy within the total contribution.

References

Ackerman, B. (1980) *Social Justice in the Liberal State*. New Haven and London: Yale University Press.

Bridges, D. (1979) *Education, Democracy and Discussion*. *Windsor*: NFER Publishing Co.

Cochrane, D., Hamm C., and Kazepides, A. (1979) *The Domain of Moral Education*. New York: Paulist Press.

Gilligan, C., Ward, J. and Taylor, J. (1988) *Mapping the Moral Domain*. Cambridge, MA: Harvard University Press.

Habermas, J. (1990a) *Moral Consciousness and Communicative Action*. Cambridge, MA: MIT Press.

Habermas, J. (1990b) 'Discourse Ethics: notes on a program of philosophical justification' in S. Benhabib and F. Dallmayr, *The Communicative Ethics Controversy*. Cambridge, MA: MIT Press.

Hare, R. (1981) *Moral Thinking*. Oxford: Oxford University Press.

Hare, R. (1992) 'Value education in a pluralist society: a philosophical glance at the Humanities Curriculum Project' in *Essays on Religion and Education*. Oxford: Oxford University Press.

Haydon, G. (1992) 'Teacher education for values education: is there a way forward under current constraints?' *Australian Journal of Teacher Education* 17 (1), pp 7-13

Haydon, G. (1993) 'Conceptions of the secular in society, polity and schools' Paper presented at the *Annual Conference of The Philosophy of Education Society*.

MacIntyre, A. (1981) *After Virtue*. London: Duckworth.

MacIntyre, A. (1987) 'The idea of an educated public' in G. Haydon (ed.), *Education and Values*. London: Institute of Education, University of London.

Patten, J. (1992) 'There is a choice: good or evil' *The Spectator*, 18 April.

Peters, R. (1981) *Moral Development and Moral Education*. London: Unwin.

Pring, R. (1984) *Personal and Social Education in the Curriculum*. London: Hodder & Stoughton.

Rawls, J. (1972) *A Theory of Justice*. Oxford: Clarendon Press.

Raz, J. (1986) *The Morality of Freedom*. Oxford: Oxford University Press.

Straughan, R. (1982) *Can We Teach Children to be Good?* London: Unwin.

White, J. (1990) *Education and the Good Life*. London: Kogan Page.

Wilson, J. (1990) *A New Introduction to Moral Education*. London: Cassell.

Changing literacies: Media education and modern culture

David Buckingham

'TV zombies', 'witless media dupes' or techno-whiz-kids? What will changing media technologies make of our children? David Buckingham argues that the proposal to remove media education from the National Curriculum for English ignores the central importance of the media in children's lives and the rise of new forms of technologically inspired literacy. The children in our schools today must inhabit the media-oriented, technical, cultural and literary landscape of the twenty-first century. We must not shrink from providing them with the competence and understanding which will enable them to inhabit this landscape with ease.

ISBN 1 872767 61 3 28 pp paperback £3.95

Partnership in teacher training: Talk and chalk

Clare Hake

Learning on the job will not produce teachers who can reflect on, compare, and thereby improve their practice. Clare Hake applauds the recent shift in emphasis towards more school-based teacher training, but argues that university departments of education can and must make a continuing contribution to training. In the space created by a partnership between school and college, students can conduct 'an active and rational exploration of the task of teaching'. Using her own experience first as a mentor for trainee teachers in school, and later as a university curriculum tutor, Clare Hake describes and illustrates the advantages of the partnership between school and college exemplified by the Oxford University teacher training scheme. School experience may be paramount but impoverished without the opportunity for reflection provided by such a partnership.

ISBN 1 872767 46 X 36 pp paperback £3.95

A market-led alternative for the curriculum: Breaking the code

James Tooley

The National Curriculum is a national disaster. But there appears to be a consensus that a national curriculum of some kind is desirable. James Tooley challenges this consensus, and argues radically that curricula should be entrusted to the market. Reviewing the arguments for a national curriculum, he concludes that a cumbersome, costly, unreliable and ultimately unnecessary, national system should be abandoned and market forces should be allowed to operate. He argues that a market-led curriculum would be liberating, empowering and facilitate egalitarian ideas far better than any bureaucratised, centralised curriculum.

ISBN 1 872767 51 6 42 pp paperback £3.95

The aims of school history: The National Curriculum and beyond

Peter Lee, John Slater, Paddy Walsh and John White with a preface by Denis Shemilt

Why is it important to include history in the school curriculum? Is it because the subject (and its methodology) is so profoundly educative that it can be engaged in for its own sake? Or should the study of the past be harnessed to purposes such as preparation for democratic citizenship? These and other questions highlighted by the introduction of the National Curriculum are discussed here by historians and philosophers. The result is a lively and stimulating debate that has important implications for the future of school history.

ISBN 1 872767 26 5 55 pp paperback £4.50

Time to change the 1981 Education Act
Brahm Norwich

Brahm Norwich reviews the workings of the 1981 Education Act and how far the special education provision it was intended to enhance has been affected by the 1988 Education Act and subsequent developments. He argues for a reassessment of the definition of special educational need and for tightening the link between assessment of need and provision. Concern for the protection of provision on changing circumstances also prompts him to recommend that duties placed on local education authorities by the 1981 Act should be now extended to school governing bodies, and that parents should have the choice of a quicker form of decision making.

ISBN 1 872767 36 2 36 pp paperback £3.95

The promise and perils of educational comparison
Martin McLean

Can Britain's relatively poor economic performance be blamed on its inferior schools and teaching? Politicians in recent years have increasingly supported their proposals for educational reform with examples of practice in other countries. Against this background Martin McLean examines the uses and possible abuses of the discipline of comparative education. He illustrates his argument with many possible examples, concluding that the challenge to those who turn to other systems of education to find support for their arguments is whether they can let their thinking 'take in deeper and wider perspectives and whether they can accept the conclusions that emerge'.

ISBN 1 872767 31 1 40 pp paperback £3.95

National Curriculum science: So near and yet so far
Arthur Jennings

When the first proposals for the National Curriculum science were published in 1988 the goal of giving all pupils a broad and exciting experience of science seemed to be within reach. Arthur Jennings traces here the history of implementation and asks whether, under pressure of accommodating a workable system of assessment, that original goal has not been lost. Teachers will need to be vigilant, he urges, and carry parents and school governors with them, if they are to go beyond teaching 'to the tests' and achieve a real experience of science for all.

ISBN 1 872767 41 9 41 pp paperback £3.95

The arts 5-16: Changing the agenda
John White

John White critically examines the central issues that underlie the National Curriculum Council's document *The Arts 5-16: A curriculum framework*. Education in the arts has lacked a coherent sense of purpose and whilst the NCC has tried to provide an integrated policy it has paid insufficient attention to the underlying aims of education in the arts. In addressing this problem John White presents a searching discussion of the purposes and underlying assumptions of education in the arts and their practical realisation. His concern is to ensure that the foundations for work in school in the arts are secure and defensible and above all will generate a love of art.

ISBN 1 872767 06 0 38 pp paperback £3.95

More has meant women: the feminisation of schooling
Jane Miller

'To an extent that is quite inadequately recognised, state education is provided by women; as is virtually all schooling, whether public or private, for young children.' Jane Miller argues that criticism of current educational practice often has gender as its hidden target. She draws on historical evidence and on her own teaching experience to develop a complex and provocative discussion.

ISBN 1 872767 21 4 31 pp paperback £3.95

Music education and the National Curriculum
Keith Swanwick

Keith Swanwick discusses the evolution of music education in schools and critically examines the implications of the attainment targets in the National Curriculum. On the central question of music as knowledge he considers that the National Curriculum Working Group put a misplaced emphasis on factual information and quantity. Knowing about and understanding music is much more than processing factual information and any form of assessment must recognise *qualitative* awareness rather than acquisition of *quantitative* facts. Swanwick's improved criteria for assessment have in part been accepted by the Secretary of State for Education. In this strongly argued work Swanwick seeks to identify a way forward for music in the classroom that would secure the confidence of musicians and music educators.

ISBN 1 872767 11 7 33 pp paperback £3.95

the Tufnell Press
47 Dalmeny Road,
London, N7 0DY

ORDER FORM

Please send me the following:

	Price	Quantity	Total

Total amount enclosed ____________

Please make cheques payable to the Tufnell Press

NAME ____________________

ADDRESS ____________________

____

____

INS9/1993